TUCSONIAN JOHN K. GOODMAN'S roster of achievements is an impressive mixture of scholarship, business expertise, sportive and social activity, and art collection and promotion. A 1942 *summa cum laude,* Phi Beta Kappa graduate of Yale University, Goodman has published articles on western art and Thoroughbreds. He is a founding member and present chairman of the board of Tucson's Mountain Oyster Club, a prestigious social organization which each year sponsors a major western art exhibition. He has also served as director and an advisory board member of the Tucson Museum of Art. An avid horse-racing fan and polo player, Goodman has served as chairman of the Arizona Racing Commission and governor of the United States Polo Association. As a businessman, he is both a real estate investor and chairman of the finance committee of a savings and loan association.

Goodman began collecting western art in 1941, and has since amassed over 250 paintings, drawings and bronzes of many prominent western artists, including, of course, Ross Stefan, his friend of many years.

ROSS STEFAN

BELOW THE MESA OF THE SUN — NAVAJO *oil, 28 x 36 inches*

ROSS STEFAN

An impressionistic painter of the contemporary Southwest

BY JOHN K. GOODMAN
with a foreword by Clay Lockett

NORTHLAND PRESS

To my wife Aline

Table of Contents

List of Illustrations

Foreword

COLLECTING western and Indian art has been a very fascinating and certainly rewarding experience for me over the last four decades. The changes I have witnessed in these past few years in attitudes among collectors, galleries, critics, and more especially the artists, have been dramatic. Back when Russell and Remington were the *only* names in western art, the opportunity for the average citizen to view their original paintings was quite limited, for the works were generally only to be found in eastern galleries or homes of the wealthy. Most likely the only general exposure the artists had was through syndication of calendars or other forms of print reproduction. As Norman Rockwell's international fame came from his cover illustrations for the *Saturday Evening Post,* so did the fame of Russell and Remington reach its largest audience through the medium of print.

Today we are fortunate to have fine, young painters like Ross Stefan. These contemporary artists have the sensitivity and talent to record the color and excitement of the western scene and are productive enough that paintings can be viewed in many public institutions, more private collections than years ago, and are generally more available to the average person interested in viewing or buying art of the West.

Ross paints with a wonderful flare for color, yet maintains authenticity of detail which documents the scene with a historical significance. He lets the violence of the world go unrecorded on his canvases — refreshing to this old man.

Many artists past and present have painted cowboys and Indians — and many, even some of the great ones, have just missed, as far as I am concerned, because they really didn't know the subject matter. The Navajo landscape would include a saguaro cactus, or the old trapper would have a modern rifle, or the wrong tribe would be doing the wrong thing — there are a variety of blatant anomalies. One of the reasons I so admire Ross Stefan is that he really does know the subjects that he paints. His cowboys and Indians are today — everything they do, wear, and use in his paintings are today, not the romantic past.

I realize that there can be artistic licence, but being a Southwest aficionado, I prefer southwestern art to be correct. I do not equate this with photocopy art or staunch realism, but rather mean that the art should invoke true impressions. When you view a Stefan painting you see the Southwest in a comprehensible, honest rendition, yet through the artist's impressionistic eye. And your insights are broadened by a very talented young man.

CLAY LOCKETT

OLD SANTA CRUZ *oil, 16 x 22 inches*

2 ROSS STEFAN

The Wauwatosa Wonder

ROSS STEFAN was born in Milwaukee, Wisconsin, on June 13, 1934. His father, Ed Stefan, had emigrated to America from Austria as a child in 1905, and grew up in Milwaukee where he eventually entered the advertising business. In 1929 he married Ross's mother, Ivah, who had emigrated to Wisconsin from Norway with her parents and homesteaded in the Long Coolee area at Holman.

Ross displayed his artistic talent early in life, and by the age of seven he had already attracted the attention of the press, as shown in this excerpt from an article in the *Milwaukee Journal* which was accompanied by illustrations of two of his drawings: "Ross Stefan may not be the greatest artist in the world for his age, but it's safe to say that he is the greatest combination artist and businessman for his age Milwaukee has ever seen. Ross is just seven years old and is in the second grade of Neskara school. Two of his hundreds of original drawings are shown here. We couldn't show any more, because he has sold them. In recent weeks he has collected more than twenty dollars — there's something for professional artists to shoot at. The reason for the excessive activity? You guessed it — he's buying defense bonds."

Obviously the reporter's attention to this subject was inspired by someone, and that someone was Ed Stefan. Ed was early aware and proud of Ross's talent. Ed by nature was and is a promoter and showman, and from Ross's formative years until he was in his early twenties he promoted Ross and his paintings however and wherever he could.

Beginning at the age of eight, Ross spent the summers with his great-uncle, Henry O. Johnson, a one-man integrated dairy in Holman, Wisconsin. Mr. Johnson possessed twenty-three golden guernsey cows which made up one of the prize herds in Wisconsin. He personally fed them, milked them, bottled their milk, and delivered it to his customers in the nearby village of Holman.

Ross fed and milked cows, mucked out manure, gathered eggs, cleaned out chicken coops and did a hundred other farm chores, besides learning to drive his uncle's Model A Ford truck to follow him along his milk route in Holman.

Ross feels that this was his first important contact with farm life and farm animals. "The days at Uncle Henry's farm have given me an intangible feeling you can't talk about of rural America, a reminder of a bygone era that has almost disappeared." Pointing out a painting of an old Arizona rancho with a horse in front of it, he notes: "I am not just off the illustrators' wagon turned to western painting. I have lived and experienced the feelings that make this kind of life." There must be much merit in his statement because the indicated painting is to be used in the 1978 Lezius-Hiles-Fine American Art Calendar Collection also containing reproductions of paintings by N. C. Wyeth, Don Kingman, Ben Stahl, and Frederic Remington — which, Ross remarks, "is good company for any artist."

The next newspaper notice of Ross Stefan's early work is from the *Milwaukee Journal,* June 11, 1947. There is a photograph of a smiling Ross — mostly teeth — at his easel with an unfinished pen-and-ink drawing that he was working on. Underneath the photo, the caption states: "Ross Stefan who will be thirteen on Friday, June 13, tried to finish thirteen western pictures for his one-boy show, to be opened on his birthday. But he couldn't find the time, although he labored prodigiously. But he has all but half of the thirteenth one done. It is the

CANYON GIRL   *oil, 18 x 24 inches*

ROSS STEFAN 5

This pastel was done in 1949, one year after young Ross made his first trip west — to the Seven Dash Guest Ranch southwest of Tucson.

A pastel done by thirteen-year-old Ross, who sneaked it into a high school art competition and won first prize.

Young Ross Stefan in his studio during his high school days in Tucson. By this time Ross had begun concentrating on the medium of oil and had joined the Artist's Professional League. PIETRO BALESTRERO, Western Ways

unfinished half of the horse in the picture you see him working on. The show will be held at his home, in Wauwatosa. He had planned to use any money made from the sale of his pastels for a western trip but has changed his mind. The money will go to the war memorial."

A few years before this, his last show in Milwaukee, Ross met Dan Muller, who was to have a definite effect on Ross's life and his desire to become a western painter.

Dan Muller was an "adopted son" of Buffalo Bill Cody. He was a painter of the West and he lived and had his studio at Port Washington, Wisconsin, a short forty-five minutes from Milwaukee. Muller, who was then in his sixties and died just last year, cottoned to young Ross and provided his first real link to the far West. Muller had traveled all over the world with the Buffalo Bill Wild West Shows, and had spent much time with his "father" both at the Nebraska ranch and later at the Cody's IRMA Hotel and Ranch in Wyoming. In Muller's studio, Ross had his first personal contact with the artifacts of the West. He still remembers vividly looking at the Cheyenne and Sioux war shields, their bows and arrows, putting on the woolly chaps of the Northwest, and holding the spurs of working cowboys in his hands. He was fascinated by the rifles and six-shooters that he saw and examined in the benevolent Muller's studio. It was there that he was to learn the difference between the double-cinched saddle of the Southwest and the center-fire stock saddle of the Northwest. As Ross says, "Up to that time, the closest I had been to anything western was the Lone Ranger on radio. We didn't have television in those days."

Dan Muller lavished time, knowledge and care on young Stefan, and Ross has characteristically always acknowledged his debt to him. If Ross has one unfailing attribute, it is his ability to cheerfully acknowledge the individuals who have helped him along his way in his forty-two years of life. He takes nothing away from these helpful beings, in

COMPADRES — PATAGONIA COUNTRY   *oil, 28 x 36 inches*

Ross Stefan has been selected Artist of the Year for 1978 by the Tucson Festival Society. The above painting was lithographed as a commemoration to the honor and is the only Stefan work to have been reproduced in a lithographed edition signed by the artist.

ROSS STEFAN 9

IO ROSS STEFAN

HAS YESTERDAY FOUND YOU? SONOITA — SOUTHERN ARIZONA   *oil, 28 x 50 inches*

ROSS STEFAN **II**

SANTO DOMINGO CLOUD DANCER   *oil, 28 x 22 inches*

fact, he may over-emphasize the part that they played in his life. He has maintained a relationship throughout the years with these, his friends of the past. He is as enthusiastic in his appreciation of their bygone efforts in his behalf as if they had taken place yesterday. Ross Stefan, although he has grown large on the western art scene, never forgets his former benefactors — an attribute that many artists have conveniently discarded once success came their way.

Before he left Milwaukee Ross was to win the *Milwaukee Journal* Student Art Calendar award in the senior high school classification. The *Journal* noted: "Youngest of the prize winners is Ross Stefan, thirteen, previously known as a cowboy artist. Ross goes to Longfellow Junior High School in Wauwatosa where his art teacher is R. A. Dawe. He sneaked into the competition — being not in senior high school as of that time. His picture shows an old-fashioned horse and buggy waiting for the family doctor who grins broadly as he comes down the walk from a front door." This pastel was entitled *It's a Boy* and shows Stefan's early attention to detail. Ross, at the age of thirteen, was already beginning to attract the trained eye of the professional, and one result of his triumph in this competition was a letter to Ed Stefan from the vice-president of a Minneapolis firm specializing in fine printing, praising Ross's rapidly developing talent and offering to introduce Ross to Norman Rockwell for professional training.

However, fate had other plans for young Ross. In 1947 Ross contracted a very serious case of pneumonia and remained in a coma for ten days. His family despaired of his life. Penicillin, the new miracle drug of that day, was used as a last resort, and Ross recovered.

Ed Stefan decided to take Ross out of the cold Wisconsin winters over the 1948–49 Christmas vacation to a warm climate — southern Arizona — and the historic Seven Dash Guest Ranch. They arrived in Arizona in the early part of January, 1948.

I4 ROSS STEFAN

ALONG WHITTLER'S CREEK   *ink drawing, 15 x 20 inches*

ROSS STEFAN 15

KENNY CLY'S WIFE *oil, 10 x 8 inches*

Early Days in Arizona

Ed AND ROSS STEFAN'S STAY at the Seven Dash Guest Ranch provided Ross his first western experience. The Seven Dash, which was also a working ranch, was located in the Little Dragoon Mountains near the Chiracahua Mountains about eighty miles southeast of Tucson. During its existence as a guest ranch, the Seven Dash catered to such diverse celebrities as President Teddy Roosevelt and Clark Gable.

In 1948, Tucson had a population of between 45,000 and 50,000 people, and was the second largest city in Arizona. It was then still partially a cow town with a strong flavor of the Old West. Howell Manning, the Gill brothers, Carlos Ronstadt, Harry Saxon, Roy Adams, Jim Converse, Tol Pendleton, and Boyd Wilson were the cattle barons of that era and figures of importance in the community. The rest of the economy depended upon winter tourism, the Southern Pacific Railroad and Davis-Monthan Airfield.

Ed Stefan announced his intent to move to Tucson by heralding in the *Arizona Daily Star* with the following article: "Young Visitor to the West to be resident soon — Ross Stefan — thirteen years old, artist of Wauwatosa, Wisconsin, who accompanied his father, Mr. Edward J. Stefan, for three weeks in January at the Seven Dash Ranch at Dragoon, Arizona, was a first prize winner in an art contest sponsored recently by the *Milwaukee Journal.*"

Ed Stefan had broken the ice for Ross in Arizona with his knowledge of public relations before his family had even moved to Tucson.

The Stefans decided to return to Tucson as soon as possible. However, this move was not a permanent one until 1949. Ed Stefan sold his advertising business in Milwaukee and settled Ross and the balance of his family in Tucson. Ross enrolled in Tucson High School, where he subsequently graduated four years later as a member of the National Honor Society. While Ross was attending Tucson High, he was busily painting in pastels, and Ed Stefan was using all his ability to get Ross one-man shows wherever possible. The first show Ross had in Arizona was in the window of Porter's Saddlery and Western Wear Store. Harold Porter, son of the pioneer founder, arranged this show for Ross in 1949. The *Tucson Daily Citizen* of 1950 noted Ross's first professional showing at the new downtown branch of the Bank of Douglas. There were also shows at the National Bank of El Paso in conjunction with the opening of the El Paso, Texas, Centennial and at the Bank of Douglas in Phoenix, Scottsdale, and Mesa.

What kind of pastels was Ross Stefan painting at the age of fifteen? At the best, passable; certainly not the kind his present-day collectors would hang on their walls to exhibit their artistic tastes. As Ross says, "I had received a great deal of 'push' through the newspapers . . . before I was ready for it." Stefan admits that some of the push from the early days is ingrained in him. "I'm still mailing out brochures," he says with a smile.

It was in 1950, at the age of sixteen, when Ross Stefan created the first painting to display a real degree of professional competence and give promise of his future abilities. The work was a pastel of San Xavier del Bac, one of the oldest missions of the Southwest, located ten miles south of Tucson along the Santa Cruz River on the edge of the Papago Indian Reservation. It was reproduced in 1952 by the Harrison-Smith Company of Minneapolis as a part of their Christmas card series for that year. This brought Ross regional as well as some national rec-

ARIVACA EVENING *oil, 16 x 22 inches*

ROSS STEFAN 19

ROSS STEFAN

THE MEDICINE MAN'S WAY — NASCHITTI CANYON   *oil, 28 x 50 inches*

ROSS STEFAN **21**

GERONIMO KNEW THIS TRAIL WELL   *oil, 28 x 36 inches*

22 ROSS STEFAN

ognition. The *Arizona Daily Star* noted that "the painting, started on Christmas Day, 1949, shows the ancient Spanish mission in early morning light with Papago Indians leaving Mass. Much of the scene could have been painted one hundred years ago, but a modern touch is a truck parked to one side."

Ross Stefan took two real strides forward in 1952. He began painting in oils for the first time, and he became a member of the American Artists Professional League. Ross's first oil painting was of the historic Bird Cage Theater in Tombstone, Arizona (now in the collection of the Arizona Pioneer Historical Society in Tucson). We find from 1953 a brochure that reads, "The Bank of Douglas is proud to present the Sixth Annual Exhibit of paintings by Arizona's popular teenage artist — Ross Stefan." This printed invitation included a photograph of a shy, smiling young Ross. We also find from the newspapers that the exhibition was a sellout. In the spring of 1953, Stefan graduated from Tucson High School and enrolled that fall in the University of Arizona. He majored in philosophy and art education. In 1953 he was hired as a part-time artist by the *Arizona Daily Star,* and his ink sketches were exclusively used in the newspaper magazine section, "The Roundup." Stefan's own recollection of his career at the university was that it was "stormy."

In the spring of 1954, Ross met his future bride, Anne Silverson, of Minneapolis. Anne, then a student at the University of Colorado, was visiting her friend Ann Mathews. This definitely was no "love at first sight." Ross recalls, "I was sitting under the grand piano in the Mathews's living room when Anne entered the room. I did not get up, but kept on talking with my friends, a tightly knit group that spent their Friday and Saturday nights at a south Tucson Mexican dance hall." Anne also admits that she was not overcome by her first meeting with the youthful artist.

It was in the winter of 1953–54 that Ross Stefan made the acquaintance of Richard Riss — a trucking magnate from Kansas City, Missouri, who wintered in Tucson, then a community of about 60,000 persons. Stefan always exhibited a painting in the window of Nick's Shoe Store, an outlet for children's shoes. Riss saw and liked the painting and obtained Stefan's phone number and address. The next day he called on Ross and, to use Stefan's words, "bought everything in the house." Seven of the paintings were to grace the 100-foot-long living room of his beautiful new lodge at Sioux Lookout, Ontario. Riss proceeded to pay for the seven paintings with eight $100 bills, the first Ross had ever handled. When he and his father delivered the paintings to Riss's private plane at the Tucson Municipal Airport Riss told him, "When you are out of school this summer, come up to my lodge at Sioux Look Out. It will broaden your perspectives and you may meet some people that you can sell paintings to. Just meet me in Kansas City, and I'll fly you up to Ontario." It was quite an invitation for a nineteen-year-old boy whose whole world up to then had been limited to parts of Wisconsin and southern Arizona.

When his school year ended, Ross climbed on the bus to Kansas City, Missouri, for his first big trip away from home. He registered into the Pickwick Hotel near the bus station, which he recalls as the "crummiest hotel in Kansas City, with one light bulb in the middle of the room." He then called Richard Riss at his farm and said, "This is Ross Stefan speaking." Riss said, "Ross who? I have never heard of you."

Stefan, bordering on desperation, described himself: "I'm the guy you bought the paintings from for your lodge in Ontario." Riss then promptly recalled Ross and his invitation. The next morning Riss's car and chauffeur picked Ross up at "the crummiest hotel in Kansas City" and took him to the Riss Building, where he met his patron.

Riss then took Ross to a large luncheon he was giving at the Kansas

THE LAST TIME I SAW THE HUNTER   *ink drawing, 20 x 15 inches*

ROSS STEFAN 25

City Club. Among the honored guests was former president Harry Truman who said, "Have a nice summer, I'm sure you'll enjoy the lodge in Canada." So awed was Ross that he couldn't get any words out to reply to the former president.

Riss, true to his word, flew Ross to his Canadian retreat for the summer. There Ross was to enjoy a dazzling spectrum of life for the first time in his youthful career. Dick Riss liked to surround himself with all types of characters and individuals, and some of them were most impressive to young Stefan. That summer Ross was to meet Teamster Jimmy Hoffa, Morris B. Sachs, the founder and owner of Sach's Men's Clothes in Chicago, Harry Mossman, the master builder of steel bridges, again president Harry Truman, who came to enjoy the Canadian fishing, and Gilbert Bartling, of Brotherhood Block in Kansas City. There was a constant flow of high-powered executives. Most of them bought paintings Ross had done which depicted the Canadian wilderness.

Ross sold several thousand dollars worth of paintings that summer, and then returned to Tucson in the fall to again attend the University of Arizona. Ross had certainly had his perspectives broadened in several ways — he was able to buy a new Buick with the funds obtained painting at Sioux Look Out, and Dick Riss, always known as a man of his word, had given Ross Stefan his first boost in the outside world. Ross has never forgotten Riss, still corresponds with him, and has seen him several times on his Cripple Creek Ranch in the years following that important summer.

Sophomore Ross Stefan was registering at the University of Arizona, and standing at the back of the line was Anne Silverson. Ross saw her there, and marched her up to his position at the front of the line so that both their registrations could be quickly over with. Anne admits this time she definitely was interested in the tall young artist.

AT PUEBLO SAN JUAN   *oil, 30 x 40 inches*

ROSS STEFAN 27

WHISPERING SPRINGS — TESHEPI   *oil, 28 x 50 inches*

ROSS STEFAN **29**

SOUVENIRS *oil, 36 x 28 inches*

30 ROSS STEFAN

This chance meeting developed into a long series of dates over the winter, and both Anne and Ross decided to marry by spring. As his romance with Anne developed, his grades diminished, and he finally quit the university.

By the spring of 1955 Ross's relationship with Anne Silverson had progressed to the point that her family had journeyed to Tucson to meet Ross. Anne's father had little understanding of western art or artists in general, and he was not impressed with the future prospects of a struggling young painter. He suggested to Ross that he continue his education and become an art teacher, a more secure approach, to be sure. Ross turned down that suggestion, painted another sellout show, and Anne, bowing to her parents' wishes, went back to work the summer in Minneapolis. Both Anne and Ross needed whatever money they could earn. They were married on July 22, 1955, in Minneapolis on their extremely small nest egg.

Anne and Ross honeymooned that summer on the Navajo Reservation, journeying as far north as the village of Kayenta. This trip was to make a lasting and very influential impression on Ross and his future painting. Kayenta and the Navajo country were much more isolated twenty years ago than they are today. There were no paved roads and certainly very few facilities for food and lodging. The Navajos were still a people very much unto themselves, and they, their land, life-style and religion made a dramatic impact on Stefan. The Kayenta honeymoon was only the first of many field trips that he and Anne were to make to Indian country, and it marked a definite milestone in Ross's career. It was after this experience in Kayenta when his paintings of the Navajo began to see, hear and feel the Navajo people. He has polished this facet over the last twenty-odd years to such a degree that few artists can catch the color, laughter, happiness and life-styles of the Navajo and Hopi as Ross does. If viewers of his Navajo paintings have seen the

Navajos at their rodeos, ceremonial sings, or wherever they gather, they find in Stefan's portrayals of these events not only physical representations, but the emotions that go with them. What can give the viewer a happier feeling than a Stefan painting of young Navajo maidens with balloons, reflecting the joy the subjects themselves displayed when the artist witnessed the event? Stefan is also capable of capturing the dignity of an Indian woman shielding herself from the sun with a colorful umbrella. Likewise, he superbly depicts the loneliness of the landscape, the bone-rattling ache and the anticipation of a Navajo family in a wooden wagon on their way to a sing (a Navajo religious ceremony). The Kayenta honeymoon was only the first of many field trips that he and Anne were to make to the reservation. Just like the San Xavier Mission pastel in 1950, and his first use of oils in 1952, his honeymoon to Kayenta in 1955 marks a definite milestone in Ross's career. In the years to come, Stefan was to develop and extend this skill to portray the Pueblo Indians of the Southwest.

Anne and Ross returned to Tucson in the late summer of 1955. Ross found himself, at twenty-one, married, out of the university, nearly out of money, and with a definite need to earn a living to provide for Anne and himself.

Besides the experience on the Navajo Reservation, he had acquired a tremendous asset in Anne. She has persevered with Ross through the hard years and the good, and certainly deserves her due as a balance wheel to Ross's personality. At the time of their marriage Ross was no longer a teenage genius. He was a man with all of a man's responsibilities, and his ingenuity in meeting and solving these problems was as interesting and complex as the artist himself.

SOUVENIRS *ink drawing, 20 x 15 inches*

ROSS STEFAN 33

READY FOR THE TRAIL AT DOS CABEZAS   *oil, 28 x 36 inches*

34 ROSS STEFAN

Tubac

ROSS AND ANNE
were not totally penurious upon their return to Tucson. Anne's grandmother had given the young couple several thousand dollars as a wed-
ding gift. They used this to buy a small house in Tucson which Ross
renovated during the balance of the summer of 1955.

Ross and artist Dale Nichols were old friends. Nichols, an older and
more experienced painter than Ross, had a definite influence on Ross's
early career. Nichols had enjoyed a great deal of success with his styl-
ized *Nebraska Red Barn* paintings in the 1940s and '50s. Dale had used
the Charles Posten houses in Tubac, Arizona, as a studio, art school and
gallery before moving to Antigua, Guatemala. The Charles Posten
houses, a series of historic old adobes, formed just the type of environ-
ment that would appeal to the young painter. Posten in the 1880s and
'90s, through a hoax, ruled or claimed to rule Arizona as the "Baron of
Arizona." He levied his own taxes, printed his own money, performed
his own marriage ceremonies and was the law of the land. Only after
lengthy judicial process were his "Spanish Instruments" of grant found
to be carefully forged fakes.

Ross wrote Dale Nichols in Antigua and asked to lease or purchase
his old studio and gallery buildings, across the plaza from Saint Anne's
Church. Nichols replied that he had sold the buildings to Mrs. Verna
Yokum, the owner of Arizona Mortuary. Stefan quickly made a call on
Mrs. Yokum. She was indeed owner of the buildings, and she said she
would lease them to Ross as a studio and gallery. She added further

35

funds to rehabilitate the buildings, as they were in some state of disrepair since Nichols's departure. One of the things that undoubtedly influenced Ross to procure these buildings as a studio and gallery was the steady increase of tourists between Tucson and Nogales; he reckoned they would have to go right by Tubac, thirty-eight miles south of Tucson, and a certain percentage would stray into this earliest Spanish presidio in southern Arizona to see what was left of the town.

If there were trying years in Ross Stefan's life, they were at Tubac from 1955 to 1959. Ross found he was not only promoting his own paintings and his studio, but also the town of Tubac, which was by then mostly ruins. Stefan had his tenth one-man show at his Tubac gallery in 1956.

There exists a photograph of Stefan surrounded by some of his works from his early Tubac period. The photograph is large enough that the viewer can see four of the works that Stefan is displaying and there is clearly very little uniformity of style or composition between any of the four. One is a reworked and larger oil of San Xavier Mission after his successful pastel of the same subject matter which had been used on the 1952 Christmas card. The second painting is a *Rider and Packhorse* — very like Dale Nichols's style in appearance — a light composition with sharp angular planes of the background mountains that Nichols was famous for. The third, a pastel, is of Saint Anne's Church in Tubac, a nice drawing that shows promise of better things to come. The fourth painting, a rodeo scene of a bucking horse rider, is very reminiscent of the Milwaukee one-boy show days, and it displays about the same quality. At this point in time, Ross Stefan was all over the map and definitely had not "gotten himself together."

Again, in overviewing Stefan's accomplishments of this period, one sees that about ten percent of his production had much artistic merit as works of art. We even find one of his invitations or cards of that period

GATHERING FOR A TAOS CEREMONY *oil, 22 x 28 inches*

ROSS STEFAN 37

titled "Ross Stefan — Illustrator" — not much of an advertisement for a youth who was someday to become an outstanding fine arts painter.

These years at Tubac for Stefan were parsimonious, but his ability to scramble, promote and achieve a degree of financial success, rather as a side effort of his paintings, were to turn a newly wed twenty-one-year-old boy into a reasonably organized twenty-five-year-old man who exhibited many desirable talents in his struggle to succeed. Experiences other than just painting provided lessons and associations that would stand Ross Stefan in good stead for the balance of his yet young life. But no one could accuse Ross of not painting during the years 1955–59. Anyone that can average over 100 paintings a year for a four-year period has to get better or get worse. Stefan's works did improve, but not at a steadily upward rate. The quality of his production was erratic, but at the end of the Tubac era, his most severe critics would have to admit his degree of competence as a painter had increased, the style of his paintings had improved, and a certain degree of color and line that we expect in a Stefan painting today were faintly beginning to emerge. It is a credit to Ross that he accomplished as much as he did as a painter during this period when we consider the bulk and pace of his other activities.

Tourists were not stopping in droves at Tubac and were stopping even less at his studio and gallery. Stefan was fully feeling the financial pressure of being head of a household. A good deal of the adventures that were to befall young Ross were brought on by luck, but Ross always had the acumen to grab the luck and put it to work whenever and wherever possible.

Ross first used his newspaper contacts in Tucson to get a multitude of articles on Tubac, its historical value as the first Spanish presidio in Arizona and its other charms. Articles appeared not only in the Tucson media, but in the prestigious *Arizona Highways* and *Ford Times* mag-

TAOS GRANDMOTHER *ink drawing, 20 x 15 inches*

azines as well. This promotion began to pay off, and more and more visitors traveled off the Nogales Highway to see the historic Church of Saint Anne, its plaza, and the presidio ruins. A minimum of these tourists stopped at his studio. Finally, Ross in desperation began to put out signs advertising the wares of his studio and art gallery. These signs attracted only a few of the visitors at first, but as the signs got bigger, so did the number of visitors to the gallery. Stefan acted as his own gallery agent and salesman.

Ross remembers that the visitors to his gallery generally stopped because they were thirsty and wanted a drink of water after the hot trip from Nogales or Tucson. While serving the water, Ross would give a running narrative he had developed on the history of Tubac and the Santa Cruz Valley. He was a one-man tour guide of the area, and after a while this speech became an automatic part of his repertoire. But his real concern was what he could sell these individuals, and for how much. He still had many of the quarter of a million postcards that Ed Stefan had printed when Ross was thirteen. After the water and historical speech, he would try to promote a five-dollar pastel. If he had no luck on this basis, he would push six of the postcards for fifty cents.

Stefan reflects that this first year taught him to be nice to everyone, because there was no way to determine by a person's outward appearance whether they were prospective purchasers of postcards, pastels or paintings.

Stefan's first substantial sale at Tubac occurred sometime in 1956. A man and wife and six children entered his studio in the spring of that year, and the man asked if Ross could give his family a drink of water. Ross obliged and set out the eight glasses. The individual and his family were roughly dressed, sweaty, and in no manner prepossessing. Ross went through his automatic tour speech, all the while thinking, "I have eight glasses to wash for nothing."

MEMORIES — GREATERVILLE, ARIZONA   *oil, 24 x 36 inches*

42 ROSS STEFAN

THERE ARE SPIRITS IN THE WIND — MONUMENT VALLEY *oil, 28 x 50 inches*

ROSS STEFAN 43

A MIDNIGHT PRAYER   *oil, 28 x 36 inches*

44 ROSS STEFAN

The head of the family, once his thirst was satisfied, began to look around Ross's gallery. He pointed to a painting hanging on the wall and asked the price. "Fifty dollars," replied Stefan, mentally noting that the frame had cost him thirty dollars, but that he was getting his bait back plus another twenty. Ross began to feel he had a "live one," and inquiry after a second painting brought a price of seventy-five dollars. Some ten or twelve inquiries later, the man had bought out everything Ross had for sale for nine hundred dollars. The latter sum represented a normal two-months' cash flow from sales, and Stefan was elated.

The big customer was Dr. Phillips, a noted Tucson pediatrician, who was returning home from a fishing trip in Guaymas, Sonora — hence the disheveled clothing and sweaty mien. There were few air-conditioned automobiles in Arizona in 1955. Dr. Phillips became not only an ardent Stefan collector, but also a lifelong friend and doctor to Ross's two sons, Jon and Gary. He was to save Gary's life as a small boy during a critical illness.

Soon after the Dr. Phillips encounter, Ross had another drop-in roadside patron. He was William C. Morrow of Swathmore, Pennsylvania, the entrepreneur of House of Nuts which operated a chain of nut shops throughout the United States. Ross went through his usual historic spiel and his waterboy activities, and proceeded up to the "pastel pitch." Bill Morrow was definitely not interested in paintings. He was interested in land or a historic building in the Tubac area. Within twenty minutes after entering Ross's studio, he wrote a check for $1,200 made out to Ross Stefan personally with the admonition, "Buy me something, kid, I'll be back in six months."

Ross was stunned. This was 1956; the country was just emerging from the post–Korean War recession, and a total stranger had given him a check for $1,200.

During the ensuing six months, Ross was able to purchase the former postmaster's house in Tubac for $1,095. When Morrow returned six months later, he was handed the deed and the change by Ross. Morrow spent several thousand dollars on the structure for renovation and moved in.

Morrow then began a love affair with the Tubac area that was to have lasting effects. He purchased historic Hacienda Otero and the remnants of its farm and ranch land along the green banks of the Santa Cruz River. From this nucleus, he created the Tubac Country Club, interesting Bing Crosby and other financial and show business notables from all over the United States in the venture. It appeared for a short while that Tubac was well on the way to becoming the "Palm Desert" of Arizona. True, Ross was to sell Will Rogers, Jr. and his wife, Collier, on Tubac, and they bought the Old Tubac Inn, which for many years before had been headquarters of the Jim Garrett Ranch. But the "jet set" crowd just didn't arrive in Tubac, and it never became another Aspen or Scottsdale.

Despite this, Bill Morrow was to render a much longer-lasting service to that community, and Ross Stefan was deeply involved in this effort. These two men interested the Arizona State Parks Association in making Tubac Arizona's first state park. Their efforts have had a lasting beneficial historical effect that far outlasted their relatively brief stay in Tubac.

Morrow was to do Stefan several more lopsided favors. North of Tubac was the Valenzuela subdivision, a conglomeration of lots that had been platted many years before. Stefan and Morrow soon acquired title to many of the lots from their Spanish-American owners through the processing of $100 bills, late evening sorties armed with gallons of tequilla, Ross's typewriter and a sheaf of quitclaim deeds. Ross states Morrow was always fair in their transactions and that for every three lots Morrow acquired he would give Ross one-half of a lot. At the cessation of this enterprise, Ross was to own nearly a quarter of this townsite — and acquire a suitable amount of notoriety with the Arizona Land Title and Trust Company.

Morrow was to do Stefan one more favor, one that led to Ross's first real financial security in his twenty-three years of life. Late one afternoon in 1957, Morrow came to the studio with the news that the 100 acres directly across the highway from Tubac in the Diablito Mountain foothills was for sale for $100 an acre or $10,000 total. This was indeed a very good buy; the hooker in the transaction was cash — $10,000 cash.

Morrow was pretty sure that Stefan did not have this amount in cash or pledgeable assets. But this was, indeed, a tantalizer for the young artist, who wracked his brains to determine where he could obtain the necessary funds. The answer came from one of Ross's part-time students. At this time Ross was an art instructor, and he had three students who paid him five dollars a week apiece. This fifteen-dollar fee, in those non-inflationary days, put the groceries on the Stefans' table weekly. Two of Ross's three students were Louise Weyenberg and her son. Her husband, Lloyd, was of the Weyenberg Shoe Company of Milwaukee, Wisconsin. At that time, Lloyd and Louise Weyenberg owned and lived on a ranch near Arivaca, about thirty-five miles west of Tubac. Telephones did not exist in this ranching area in 1957. Soon after Morrow left, Ross decided the Weyenbergs were his only means of raising the money to buy the 100 acres across the highway from Tubac. He relates, "I jumped in my car and covered those thirty-five miles to the Weyenbergs' Arivaca Ranch at ninety miles an hour."

The Weyenbergs were leaving for Europe the next day for three months. After Louise Weyenberg had calmed Ross down and given him a drink, she learned the details of the transaction and the terms which were impossible for Ross to satisfy. She walked into her bedroom, made a check out to Ross Stefan for $10,000, told Ross to buy the land, and she and her family set sail for Europe to enjoy a three-month vacation. Ross returned to Tubac feeling airborne that evening.

The next day he called Josephine Bailey, a southern Arizona broker who was familiar with the ground. She agreed that the 100 acres was indeed a good buy at $100 per acre, and to everyone's surprise, including his own, Ross Stefan took title to the land directly across the Nogales Highway in the Diablito Mountain foothills.

No sooner had the transaction been recorded, and Stefan returned to earth, than Sid Cedargreen, a landscape painter from Wickenburg, appeared in Stefan's studio. He inquired of Ross if he knew of any land for sale in the Tubac area; just about twenty acres would be what Cedargreen needed. Ross hustled him up to the back twenty acres of his newly acquired estate. Cedargreen immediately liked the twenty-acre viewsite of the Santa Cruz Valley and inquired the price. Five hundred an acre or $10,000 for the twenty, demanded young Stefan, and he tremblingly added, "cash." Cedargreen allowed that neither the price nor the terms were any problem, and the deal shortly closed thereafter with a check being drawn to a very elated Ross Stefan.

Ross had now procured for his benefactors, who were still in Europe, the entire purchase price of the land in cash and still had eighty acres intact. He also hoped that his erstwhile art students would see fit to reward him with a finder's fee.

Europe paled on the Weyenbergs in somewhat less than three months, and they were back at their ranch in Arivaca some seventy days later. As soon as Ross heard of their arrival, he rushed over to the ranch, returned the $10,000 received from Cedargreen — and the title to the eighty acres. Mrs. Weyenberg was very pleased with the prompt return of the money within so short a period of time. She knew that

RAMONA — SANTA FE   *oil, 28 x 36 inches*

ROSS STEFAN 49

50 ROSS STEFAN

BENEATH THE CHANTS OF A THOUSAND KACHINAS   *oil, 28 x 50 inches*

ROSS STEFAN 51

OLD RED BEARD — THE TRADER — UP LATE TONIGHT *oil, 32 x 42 inches*

52 ROSS STEFAN

Ross and Anne were a young couple starting out life with very few assets. She acknowledged that Ross had performed extremely well and divided the eighty acres between Stefan and herself. It was a magnificent finder's fee, and Stefan has never forgotten the Weyenbergs' generosity and kindness.

The land acquisition was a welcome windfall, particularly welcome in that Anne was pregnant that winter with their first son, Jon. Ross was soon to sell the entire forty-acre tract for $16,000. This sum, plus funds derived from the sale of their small home in Tucson, allowed Anne and Ross to build a modest adobe home and studio in the exclusive Catalina foothills north of Tucson.

Ross's romance with Tubac still had one more flutter. He and Sid Cedargreen planned and built a studio and gallery across the plaza from Saint Anne's Church; undoubtedly Stefan supplied the plans and Cedargreen the money. The studio was large — ninety feet long by fifty feet wide. It is still one of the largest buildings in Tubac. It was completed in 1959. Stefan and Cedargreen had great difficulty in properly lighting the building to show the paintings exhibited to advantage. In their quest for help, they called upon Ivan Rosequist, the owner of Tucson's most prestigious art gallery and a very knowledgeable art dealer. Rosequist had known Ross for a number of years, as he had framed numerous paintings for him.

At that time, in 1958, Rosequist's was the only gallery worthy of designation as a gallery in Tucson. Ivan handled works of art by Remington, Russell, Sharp, Couse, Borein, Weighorst, N. C. Wyeth, and other greats. He was a keen student of western art, and was interested in what Stefan and Cedargreen were doing in Tubac. He drove down to help them with their lighting problems in their new gallery.

While remedying the studio's electrical problems, Rosequist got a firsthand all-encompassing tour of the paintings that Stefan had done over the last two years, and he liked what he saw. Ivan Rosequist had always had the ability to discover real talent in a budding artist, and he sensed that the twenty-four-year-old Stefan was a real comer. Rosequist also had the ability to promote the young artist in spheres far removed from Tubac and Tucson.

Rosequist further recognized the fact that Stefan would never develop as a competent professional artist as long as he was occupied by working as a civic promoter, a studio and gallery proprietor, an art teacher, a real estate salesman, and a dozen other vocations. Ivan realized what Stefan needed was financial security and the seclusion of a studio where he could paint unhindered.

Rosequist was not able at that time to provide the necessary annual funds to give Stefan the needed security. He approached two extremely well-known collectors about providing finances for Stefan.

Stefan signed a ten-year exclusive contract with Rosequist with Harry Bell setting up a fund to finance the contract. There was a provision in the contract that a certain percentage of the funds realized from Ross's sales over the ten-year period were to inure to Harry Bell. The plan worked, as the artist's sales were always ahead of advances provided by this fund and contract. Ross Stefan was financially assured of an annual income. He could now devote all his time to his art, and, if his artistic talent was to truly blossom, this type of discipline and devotion to painting alone was sorely needed. The personal promotion days were behind him.

In Ross's scrapbook covering the period 1959–71 he has printed in his own hand: "May 10, 1959 — Signed a Ten Year Contract with Rosequist Gallery — Tucson — Exclusive Representatives — We build a small house and studio in the Santa Catalina Mountain Foothills North of Tucson. My Tubac struggle has ended. From this date on my total production has been sold."

While Stefan had left Tubac, Tubac had left a definite mark on Stefan. His experience there represented four years of arduous struggle to survive artistically and financially. Beyond that, however, his life in Tubac exposed him to some outstanding members of the American financial community as well as the usual middle-class, everyday tourist. Stefan survived by "being nice to everyone," a trait he has assiduously followed in his public life as an artist.

If he was to learn this degree of self-security in Tubac, he was to learn far more about the countryside, its history, its inhabitants and its ruined or semi-ruined adobe buildings. The Santa Cruz Country, Arivaca, and the Sonoita, Elgin, Patagonia country that he became familiar with in those Tubac years abound in his paintings then and today. It was this era of his life that brought the old weathered barns, the battered adobes, and the beautiful old haciendas and arched missions to Stefan's paintings, and some twenty years later these subjects still are the basic background for many of his works.

Ross says of this period: "If during those years I was to meet no other person than José Guatican, an ancient Yaqui Indian who still lives in the adobe mill house on the Santa Cruz River, it would have been worthwhile. Guatican still remembers the last Apache raids on Tubac, and all this background as far as being a painter has had something to do with my feeling for the people of the land, how the sunlight bounces off an old adobe and firsthand insight on the vast country of the Southwest." Ross also acknowledges that his association with William Morrow, the godfather of Tubac, the Lloyd Weyenberg family, Collier and Will Rogers, Jr., and Sid Cedargreen, made a great impression upon an extremely formative period of his life, both as a painter and a person.

ADOBE SANTIAGO   *oil, 16 x 22 inches*

The Return to Tucson

ON MAY, 1959, the Stefans returned to Tucson for good, and Ross set up his studio in the Catalina foothills. The Rosequist Gallery's first sale of Stefan's paintings to the actor, Raymond Burr, was headlined in the *Arizona Daily Star* of September 6, 1959.

Olaf Wieghorst was recognized by the era's collectors and critics alike as a painter on the threshold of artistic greatness. Time has proved this assumption to be correct, because at the age of seventy-eight Wieghorst is considered to be the "dean emeritus" of western painting. The Rosequist Gallery handled some of Wieghorst's paintings in the late 1950s and early 1960s, and Ross came into immediate contact with these paintings at the gallery. He was impressed by them, not only by their composition and color, but by the ready saleability of the paintings and the prices (which Ross considered high) that they were bringing. He readily admits today that he was hungry and desperate to succeed, and this appeared to be an avenue to success.

Stefan adopted Wieghorst's realistic style and sophisticated palette, and continued painting in this manner for several years to come. It proved to be financially successful, but certainly not soul satisfying.

Ross notes that "with these paintings, I was being cautious. I had a family to support. . . . It is a hard process for an artist to grow." From 1960 to 1963, Ross admits he was fighting for artistic and financial survival. One sees many different phases and influences of his earlier painting styles during this period.

By late 1963, however, Ross Stefan had definitely established the basic subject matter and method as to composition, color, line and palette that were to evolve into his present-day style of painting. Stefan had by this time found the four geographical areas that he would explore artistically again and again in the years to come.

Stefan's growth to artistic maturity was closely followed by success. In 1960 his first exhibition in California at the Beverly Hills galleries of Raymond Burr was a sellout, and that same year Ivan Rosequist established a market place for Stefan's work in New Mexico at the Santa Fe gallery, The Shop of the Rainbow Man, owned by Mr. and Mrs. Hal Windus. And in 1963, the prestigious Thomas Gilcrease Institute obtained seven of Stefan's paintings through a donation by a private collector.

Ross's family life was also developing rapidly during this period, and in 1964 Anne gave birth to their second son, Gary.

In contrast to his slightly frenzied Tubac period, Ross's activities at this time were confined primarily to the studio and to field trips. He was spending, as he still does, eight hours a day in the studio with little outside socializing. This devotion to work began to bring concrete rewards by the end of 1967.

In October of that year the Panhandle Plains Historical Museum of Canyon, Texas, had an exhibition of Ross Stefan's work from private collections. There were some high-powered collectors included in this list: Raymond Burr of Hollywood; K. W. Couse of Taos, New Mexico; the Harmsens of Wheatridge, Colorado; W. C. Kurtz of Colorado Springs; and Clay Lockett of Flagstaff, long known as one of the most knowledgeable of Arizona's collectors. Ross Stefan had attracted the true long-time collectors of western art just before its popularity bubble was to strike the art world.

Ross's painting continued to improve. In the paintings of this period

ECHOES OF COCHISE   *oil, 24 x 36 inches*

ROSS STEFAN 59

there is an increasing looseness of style, the bright colors, the refined palette, and the refined use of light and shadow that are found in a Stefan painting today. By the mid-1960s, he had developed an art style that was uniquely his own.

Stefan continued to travel frequently during this period, spending his summers in Carmel, California, and visiting sites throughout the Southwest.

Ross's work was not only appreciated by his coterie of collectors but by his peers, his fellow painters in the western art world. The Cowboy Artists of America was founded in 1965. The organization was to become famous, successful, and financially powerful. Ross was invited to join the newly formed CAA by the late Charlie Dye, the organization's vice-president. In his invitational letter to Ross, Dye wrote, "I have seen your paintings both in Taos and down at Rosequist's in Tucson, and I sure like them. You are probably the youngest of the whole bunch and ought to go the farthest."

Ross declined to join the CAA. He is not a cowboy, and never has been. He knows how to ride a horse, has been around cattle, but his agricultural endeavors have been limited to his boyhood Wisconsin summers on his great-uncle's dairy farm, and a few weeks on the Seven Dash Ranch. Ross has never criticized the Cowboy Artists of America; he respects the organization and the work of many of the members. But basically Stefan has never been a "joiner."

A more significant reason for his refusal to join the CAA, however, is his feeling that an artist's competition exists within himself as motivation to improve his paintings, and is not a competition with other artists for prizes and awards.

In 1968, Jane Rosequist's ailing health prompted the decision to sell the gallery to Ralph and Dorothy Wollheim from New York City. From that date of sale, nine years ago, it has been known as Wollheims'

TAOS INDIAN *dry brush, 13 x 9½ inches*

ROSS STEFAN 61

Rosequist Galleries. Ralph and Dorothy Wollheim were typical New Yorkers. Dorothy had had some contact with the art world through her brother, the internationally known art dealer, A. M. Adler. Ralph, then in his late fifties, had been a stockbroker on Wall Street, operated a fine silver and antique shop, and had been the vice-president and sales manager for a national manufacturer of automobile accessories. The Wollheims came as a distinct shock to Stefan. He simply did not know how he would get along with the New York salesmen. Ralph, before he purchased the Rosequist Gallery, had not been a student of western art, but he rapidly acquired a deep knowledge of the field. His keen eye became trained to discern between the "good" and the "bad" of western painters and sculptors. He also rapidly acquired a reputation both with collectors and artists for scrupulous honesty. Wollheim properly represented a painting to a prospective buyer for what it was, and he paid the artists promptly when their work was sold, unlike the practices of some other galleries.

A real clue to Wollheim's personality is his desire to learn and to be successful. As an example, in 1970 this fresh-from-New-York-and-Chicago dude was invited on the five-day 100-mile *Los Charros del Desierto* ride based primarily in the Sonoita-Patagonia area that Stefan paints so proficiently. Ralph accepted, and discovered over the five days that a cowboy and horseman he was not, and had bruises and blisters to prove it. The following summer found Ralph and Dorothy attending as students the internationally famous riding school at San Miguel de Allende in Mexico. This sixty-year-old-plus student returned to Los Charros the following year as a much more capable and comfortable horseman. In the ensuing years, Ralph has applied the same will and determination to learn, plus his ability as a superb salesman to make his gallery one of the most prestigious in Arizona.

But change was in the air. Ross Stefan had his last show at the old

SAINT DOMINIC'S DAY — SANTO DOMINGO   *oil, 50 x 28 inches*

64 ROSS STEFAN

FIESTA — SAN BUENAVENTURA, CALIFORNIA   *oil, 24 x 36 inches*

ROSS STEFAN 65

OLD SANTA CRUZ — SONORA, MEXICO   *oil, 16 x 22 inches*

66 ROSS STEFAN

Rosequist Galleries at 18 South Convent Street in 1970. This old adobe building in downtown Tucson was condemned and demolished in 1971 to provide access to a new civic center. Wollheim had to move quickly, and he purchased an empty rambling building at 2843 North Campbell Avenue in North Tucson and converted it into a gracious, spacious gallery that has ultimately proven to be an extremely favorable location.

The year 1970 brought several signal tributes to Ross. A Stefan painting entitled *Line Camp* appeared in the September issue of *Western Horseman,* a magazine nationally known to those interested in the equestrian world. The October, 1970, issue of *Arizona Highways* magazine carried an illustrated article entitled "The West as Seen by Ross Stefan." A quote from the article indicates the direction that Stefan had pursued: "Stefan is regarded as a true artist of the Southwest. He paints it as he sees it without reference to the imaginary scenes of the legendary Old West. Yet one has the feeling these paintings might have been done any time in the last hundred years, so well do they convey the romance that lingers on."

By 1971 Stefan had developed that degree of competence that is the hallmark of a mature artist, and from that time on his work has displayed a uniform excellence in technique and quality.

Realization of this excellence prompted the following statement from Senator Barry Goldwater: "One of the biggest mistakes I have made in my long years of collecting western art has been that I did not early enough recognize the genius of Ross Stefan and acquire more of his paintings before that recognition was seen by so many others. He truly depicts our Southwest."

In January of 1971, Ross was one of about twenty artists to exhibit in the Mountain Oyster Club's First Contemporary Western Art Show. The Mountain Oyster Club is a longtime Tucson club composed principally of ranchers and horsemen. The organization prides itself on

TRAIL TO KAYENTA   *ink drawing, 15 x 20 inches*

retaining and preserving the traditions of the Old West. The club has held its annual art show once a year ever since. Three of Ross Stefan's paintings hang in the clubhouse along with the works of such artists as Olaf Wieghorst, Tom Ryan, William Whitaker, Robert Knudson, Clarence McGrath, Bob Lee and Bill Shaddix. All of these men are honorary artist members of the Mountain Oyster Club, and have been chosen for this distinction by the club's board of directors for excellence in the field of western art from among the forty-odd artists who have exhibited at the annual shows. And, although Ross is no joiner, he also became an honorary artist member of the club in 1973, the second artist to be chosen by the directors for this honor.

In the December, 1971, issue of *Arizona Highways,* seven full pages were devoted to Ross Stefan. The article was titled "Praised Be a Man Named Ross Stefan," and editor Joe Stacey had the following to say:

> The West of today has no more expressive painter than Ross Stefan, an artist who truly understands the land and the people of the southwest country where he has lived and worked for almost a quarter of a century. He has distinguished himself by glorifying the commonplace things of the everyday West — cowboys, horses, the Indian, mountains and ranch scenes. His paintings portray the peaceful way of life — no shoot-ups, no stage holdups, no long-horns, rodeos or cattle drives of yesteryear.
>
> Ross Stefan lives and works in Tucson, and we are proud to present this young artist who has to be ranked as one of the masters in this golden age of expressionists of the American West.
>
> His works are in every significant collection and his shows are sell-out in the foremost galleries of the Southwest. With his first major showing scheduled for the Grand Central Art Galleries in New York, in mid-January, followed by bookings across the nation, it's a sure bet that the best of the West of Ross Stefan is yet to be seen.

CAPTAIN DE ANZA LINGERED HERE   *oil, 24 x 36 inches*

ROSS STEFAN 71

72 ROSS STEFAN

COME AND BE BLESSED TWILIGHT CEREMONY — TAOS   *oil, 24 x 48 inches*

ROSS STEFAN 73

WATCHING THE SHOW AT THE SEBA DALKAI RODEO   *oil, 32 x 42 inches*

74 ROSS STEFAN

Ross was definitely in the right place at the right time. Western art had finally become fashionable, not just to the longtime devoted collectors, but also to a much wider portion of America's population. Ross's devoted concentration to his muse over the past thirty-five years was to pay off handsomely in the years to come.

In January of 1972, Ross Stefan had his first show at the prestigious Grand Central Galleries which was arranged by Ralph Wollheim. Excerpts from the *New York Times* article of January 20, 1972, state: "The Grand Central Art Galleries are presenting the paintings of a young western artist, Ross Stefan, in his first exhibition in New York. In the excellent paintings of cowboys, Indians and magnificent scenery, the artist captures the essence of the southwestern part of the United States. . . . The paintings of the Indians are extremely well done and reflect the sensitivity of the artist. . . . These [paintings] are wonderful interpretations of all the beauty of a fast-vanishing way of life and simultaneously evoke the rugged independence that makes it unique. In his first New York show, *Ross Stefan has made a splendid debut.*"

And Erwin S. Barrie, then the director and manager of the Grand Central Galleries, noted in a letter to Ralph Wollheim: "The more I look at the Ross Stefan paintings, the more favorably I am impressed with his ability as an artist. I really believe that he could eventually be on an equal footing with some of the great western painters I have promoted, such as Frank Tenney Johnson, William R. Leigh, Charlie Russell and others."

Ross Stefan had really arrived as a painter of western art, and just to prove it, his March show at Wollheims' Rosequist Galleries in 1973, which consisted of thirty-three paintings, sold out at the preview.

Further recognition was to come Ross's way in the next year. The September, 1973, issue of *American Artist* carried a feature article titled "Ross Stefan: The Development of a Prodigy," written by Frederic

Whitaker, a distinguished watercolorist himself and a member of the National Academy. In this article Stefan restates one of the basic tenets of his painting: "I see plenty of remnants of a bygone year, but I paint only what exists today. I am not trying to be a replica in miniature of the great Charles Russell." He also describes his painting techniques:

I don't know how other artists paint or what the customary routine is. I just paint the way I have worked it out. I start with a primed canvas painted in a flat, overall light or dark, warm or cool, neutralized color and then work up and down from that, starting with my darks and then leading up to the lights. I make no preliminary composition sketches or line drawings on the canvas but begin working with brush and color directly on the canvas.

Virtually all my painting is done in the studio, from ideas and notes carried in my head. Beginning with the most important component, the various picture parts are roughly painted in and then worked out in detail as I see that the composition is coming to life satisfactorily. If the composition is poor, I simply scrape out the offending members and paint in new forms until I am satisfied. For detail I sometimes refer to pencil or ink notes that I have made in the field, but those are seldom carefully rendered and are simple reminders for me of material that I consider interesting. I paint fast, and I don't hesitate to discard unsuccessful canvases. I am a firm believer in the importance of the first glance at a picture. Usually I can tell in a split second whether it is successful or lacking in some manner. If the composition is wrong, I study it until the fault reveals itself.

Whitaker describes the artist at work:

Stefan paints seated in a chair before his vertical canvas. His studio is north-lighted. Diagonally behind him is a large standing mirror that enables him with a backward glance to view his work from a distance. Beginning at seven o'clock in the morning he paints continuously, without lunch, until about four o'clock in the afternoon. By that time he is, as he puts it, 'hypnotized, from eye activity, and afraid to look, and more or less benumbed physically.' Without rising, he reaches out to grasp the handle of a set of antique altar chimes, gives it a shake, and awaits results.

The results arrive in the form of Mrs. Stefan, who seats herself in a chair carefully placed for perfect viewing, at his right and rear, and gives the artist her critique. From this he decides whether or not he should revise the work. Mrs. Stefan also intercepts callers, by phone or in person, who might disturb the artist.

Stefan has stated, "Life and painting are inseparable for me. Painting comes first, even before my family"; then he adds with a twinkle in his eye, "I am a lousy husband and a lousy father."

His paintings during this period have become much looser as to delineation, and he has developed his use of light and shadow to a much finer degree. Stefan's paintings more and more are becoming more impressionistic in an evolutionary, not a revolutionary, manner.

In 1973, Ross and Anne decided that Tucson had become too large for them. The Stefans sold their home of fourteen years in the Catalina foothills and in October moved to the Ojai Valley in central California. They purchased a home and stayed there exactly three months, returning to Tucson on December 30, content to be back in the desert.

The Stefans, upon their return to Tucson, purchased a partially completed home in the historic Tanque Verde area on the far east side of Tucson almost at the foot of the Rincon Range. Their residence is called "Chili Flats" because many years before, the land where the Stefans' home stands was a field devoted solely to the raising of chili peppers. The beauty of the Catalina Mountains to the north and the Rincons to the east dominate the skyline, and the Stefans have breathtaking views of both ranges from their home and his studio, which are well hidden in a dense grove of lovely old mesquite trees.

Besides moving back to Tucson and building Chili Flats in 1974, Ross was deeply involved in the painting world. He exhibited again at New York City's Grand Central Galleries in January. *Host* magazine, a New York publication, commented on the exhibition by stating: "For anyone in the U.S.A., these paintings of our western heritage are an exciting unique experience."

In 1975 Ross Stefan also participated in the *Up With People* Christmas card collection with twelve other distinguished artists, including Peter Hurd and Fritz Scholder.

Ross Stefan's 1975 show at Wollheims' Rosequist Galleries was another sellout. And in June of that year Ross appeared in the pages of *Arizona Highways* with an article titled "Through Indian Country with Ross Stefan." The seven paintings reproduced in that article clearly displayed the degree of perfection Stefan had reached as an impressionistic artist. The conclusion of a very successful year came with Ross being included in one of the greatest western art shows held in the last fifty years in New York at the Grand Central Galleries. With his work exhibited in the company of such great artists as Harold Von Schmidt, Nick Eggenhofer and Olaf Wieghorst, it was clear that Ross Stefan had finally achieved the recognition he truly deserves.

All of Ross Stefan's life revolves primarily around his art. His home and studio are simply an extension of his paintings. They are located in an area near the Reddington Road which allows him to get to the Happy Valley, Ash Creek, Patagonia, San Pedro, and Santa Cruz areas with a minimum amount of travel. Stefan is well known for his paintings of the cottonwoods, aspens and more especially the sycamores that are important elements of these beautiful landscapes.

Stefan knows the country he likes to paint: the Santa Cruz and San

HOW LONG HAVE I KNOWN YOU, OH CANYON?
A HUNDRED YEARS? YES. *oil, 50 x 28 inches*

80 ROSS STEFAN

THE MEDICINE MAN'S HOGAN — DENNEHOTSO WINTER *oil, 28 x 50 inches*

ROSS STEFAN 8I

AT SONOITA CREEK   *oil, 28 x 50 inches*

82 ROSS STEFAN

Pedro valleys of southern Arizona, the Catalina and Rincon mountains, the Sonoita-Patagonia area, the northern Arizona Indian reservations, and the Upper Valley of the Rio Grande from Santa Fe to Cripple Creek, Colorado. Ross notes that Andrew Wyeth painted most of his paintings within a twenty-mile radius of Chadd's Ford, and his brother-in-law, Peter Hurd, within a fifty-mile radius in the Hondo Valley and the New Mexican plains. Along with Stefan, these artists have the rare ability to convey basically the same subject matter again and again in a totally different aspect. Stefan doesn't enjoy painting the "lily pinks or the baby blues" of middle Arizona, nor does the stark bleakness of the Papago Reservation stretching along the Arizona-Mexican border from Sells westward interest his artistic sense.

Stefan feels that the development of his present style first began around 1964. His interest was and still is in light, but his work became more and more impressionistic compared to the realistic approach he had earlier adopted. In the past decade Stefan has become greatly concerned with the feeling that his painting conveys, and he refuses to subjugate the overall spirit and sense of his art to the artificial realism that many artists impose on their work. Stefan is dedicated to taking his art beyond the level of mere illustration and endowing both it and the viewer with a heightened awareness of the world he portrays on canvas. He is constantly exploring newer, more meaningful ways to render his subject matter. An example of this quest can be seen in a painting from his most recent show at Wollheims' titled *Monument Valley from Hunt's Mesa*. Ross has done three paintings from this vantage point, the first one having been completed around 1966. It is a very realistic painting with two Navajo figures on horseback in the foreground. It is a tight painting, the colors are somewhat muted, and the dominant theme of the composition centers around the Navajos. The second painting, done in 1973, is considerably looser and more impressionistic.

84 ROSS STEFAN

RANCHO SAN PEDRO *ink drawing, 15 x 20 inches*

ROSS STEFAN 85

The colors are brighter. There are still the Navajo figures on horseback, but they are more woven into the background landscape of Monument Valley, becoming a part of the whole pattern of the painting. The last painting, done in 1976, has no figures in it at all. It is a quiet abstract landscape and its color values are primarily the earth tones that one finds in a vegetable-dye Navajo rug. In 1973, Frederic Whitaker defined Stefan's work thusly: "His pictures, in general, might be called landscapes with animals. At times the animals, or human figures, dominate the scene, while the landscape is secondary — simply a note to localize the activity. On other occasions the beauty or uniqueness of the terrain is the *raison d'être* of the picture, with figures introduced to provide scale or human interest." These three paintings give a true indication of the direction Stefan has been moving toward in the last ten years.

Again, Stefan has evolved into an impressionistic painter. The essence of impressionism, he feels, is "nothing but a fleeting glimpse, and right away everything appears in order. Look at Fechin's work, nothing is in detail, but you have the feeling that it's all there, but it isn't."

"I am a firm believer in the first glance. If something about a painting does not grab you, there's probably something wrong with it.

"If it's right, it all falls into place. We've all lived enough life to know how sunlight comes through the window and strikes the interior, even if it's subconscious. A leaf has a softer edge and a sharper one. If the sharp edge is soft, something is out of whack. It either clicks or doesn't, and I know it intrinsically."

Stefan admits he is very impatient and once he starts something, he has to get it finished. He finishes each project separately. "Each painting is a life in itself, and a life itself. I don't have several paintings going at once. There is no way for me to intertwine it with five other paintings. If I can't finish it, I wipe it out, I destroy it."

Stefan works on a theory similar to that utilized for centuries by certain schools of Chinese painters, who might contemplate the blank canvas for many hours before actually beginning the painting in order to fully develop it in their minds. Stefan as well will stare at a canvas for hours on end before starting to actually paint. "I never go into the studio in the morning and know what I am going to come up with or what I am going to do. An artist's entire life goes into each painting, and while I'm able to get a painting pretty well wrapped up in a day I might take a week or longer deliberating on it, adding only a stroke or so during that time. It's not finished until I am satisfied with it."

Stefan believes that the taste of collectors evolves towards more impressionistic art as it grows in maturity and sensitivity. He also notes that some of the finest work done by artists considered to be masters in the western genre, Remington and Russell, for instance, was definitely impressionistic. On the other hand, Ross observes, many painters of the Taos School lacked the looseness that marks impressionism.

> Many of the Taos School were foreign born or foreign trained. Sharp, Berninghaus, Fechin and Couse were all National Academians — so were Frank Tenney Johnson and Frederic Remington, though not of the Taos School. There is a great difference between the National Academy members and the other artists in that Taos School, the academicians were formula painters; they had a regular set way to break down a canvas. The same thing rings true throughout their paintings. They used the same spacial breakdowns, and the same value and color theory. You can't lose on it, if you follow it, because it most always works. I stay away from it (the formulas). You find yourself in a rut, turning out little productions. Rules are made to be broken in this game — you can't teach painting. Painting can't be taught or talked about. You can teach elementary drawing, anatomy, and perspective, but again *yon can't teach painting*.

Ordinarily I go into the studio with a free spirit for the day. Don't be bogged down with all kinds of rules, otherwise you wind up a machine producing a product.

The gradual evolution of Stefan's art toward the impressionistic has been very deliberately developed and nurtured, and the result is the mastery one finds in his canvases today. Ross projects on the directions he would like to pursue.

"I would like to simplify my life, paint a little less. I would like to simplify my painting, concentrate on developing with a little more independence. Take more chances. I'd like to do more 'far out' paintings — but not on a tangent as many artists do. I'd like to explore the avenue of camouflaging my subject in the painting. Make the viewer work harder, perhaps have more fun discovering the painting, and once they find it, it will be a delightful surprise — if I can pull it off.

"Let me give you an example of an artist taking a chance. The subject matter of my 1976 show at Wollheims' gallery was all Indians. Ralph had some concern over the saleability of the thirty-odd paintings if all of them were to be of Indians — or Indian subject matter. I thought it was a great idea for a bicentennial show. Incidentally, it was a sellout."

A "take a chance" idea for 1977 was to paint the old Greaterville (Arizona) schoolhouse — "I mean the interior of a deserted school. Did you ever see Ross Stefan paint a deserted school?" The *Greaterville Schoolhouse* was a feature painting in the 1977 show; naturally, it was sold.

One more facet must be added to any book on Ross Stefan as an artist, and that is his absolute antipathy in entering any shows or galleries where awards are given. As stated earlier, he feels continuing improvement is a contest within the artist himself — and not a contest

Ross Stefan relaxes outside his studio in the Tanque Verde area of Tucson. From the studio, one can view both the Catalina and Rincon mountain ranges of southern Arizona.
JARVIS HARRIMAN, Tucson Festival Society

with other artists. Nothing bears this out more clearly than a series of letters between Dean Krakel and Stefan on the merits and demerits of the National Academy of Western Art and the artists' competitions held at the Cowboy Hall of Fame. In a letter to Krakel on July 9, 1975, Ross wrote, "Perhaps for a non-artist, it is difficult to understand that any art that is worthwhile must reflect the life of the artist, not the critic, committee, or jury! An artist competes with himself. This is probably the most difficult kind of competition there is. If an artist is to be a rising star in life — standards — incentives — inspirations and last but not least — ability — all must grow from within the artist. Art is personal. In the history of art, talking above the elementary, it's easy to find that the painters that lasted came about in the above-mentioned way."

These hardly resemble the words of the Ross Stefan who one meets at his one-man shows. Ross is genuinely a shy man with multitudes of people. He is polite, cool, somewhat taciturn and rather uncommunicative. But behind Stefan's cool public exterior burns a soul that readily expresses its thoughts on canvas. To his intimates he voices, speaks and writes his opinions on almost any given subject. And his words are powerful.

A portion of Krakel's reply, written July 16, 1975, reads: "The Cowboy Hall of Fame (Dean Krakel) competes. . . . Like Ross Stefan, I am competing with myself, to see if we can't create an unbelievably great institution that will affect through a quality sense in art, rodeo performance, book, magazine, and film, the lives of millions. So they will appreciate our American history through different media. There are no prizes for such achievements, only pride and satisfaction. Two big things we will take with us to the happy hunting grounds. You will leave a fine legacy of paintings."

The totally unique and wide catholicism of his collectors is the result of Stefan's style of painting. He is a self-taught artist with few outside influences, and he imitates no one. Through the years he has developed in his paintings a combination of pattern, color, composition and subject matter that gives the viewer a feeling of lightness and clarity, and at the same time conveys a dynamic sense of happiness and pleasure. As a master colorist, Stefan is one of the few western artists who can produce a third dimension in painting solely by the use of color. These characteristics are evident throughout all Stefan's paintings, be they landscape, portrait, or animated action. It is a non-imitative Stefan trademark.

Among Stefan's many honors has been his recent selection by the art committee of the Tucson Festival of Arts as 1978 Artist of the Year. With this he joins an exclusive group of western artists which includes Olaf Wieghorst, Paul Dyck, Fred Kabotie and James Reynolds.

Time alone will tell what further development awaits Stefan and his paintings; certainly he will continue to grow as a painter and as a person. His paintings, while continuing to bring a sense of happiness and pleasure to the viewer, will reflect the ever-growing maturity of Stefan — the artist and the man.

THIS BOOK
WAS DESIGNED BY PAUL WEAVER,
SET IN GRANJON TYPES WITH BEMBO DISPLAY
AND PRINTED ON SHASTA GLOSS.
BINDING WAS BY
ROSWELL BOOKBINDING.